GW00384037

written by
Jason Phillips

illustrated by
Norris Nuvo

foreword by
Cai Hughes

edited by
Eleanor Burns

layout by
Paul Bevan

title graphic by
Laure Lajarthe

tantrumbooks.co.uk

© TANTRUM 2015

CHAV PUNK HOBBIT

The Quest to the End of the World

For lovely Annie

CONTENTS

FOREWORD

Looking back I think it's fair to say the author of this book has provided some seminal moments in my creative development. My first memory of Jason was at a night out in the Lakota club Bristol. It must have been circa 1995. House music was the staple diet and all of my peers were consuming it as voraciously as the little white pills that were so prevalent.

But I was unconvinced. Not by the technical merits but by my affinity with the people and the music.

I remember during that post club slump in his parents living room, Jason fizzed about an Oliver Stone biopic and its protagonist Jim Morrison of The Doors.

The light flashed on. The levers clanged and the tracks of my musical lineage were switched for good. I guess we picked up from there and our relationship grew through some common creative interests in film and music and our aspirations to tear through the ceiling of our council estate raising and burn our way up and out.

The second and more salient keystone came in the guise of a bitten eared and buckled book he thrust into my hand accompanied with his trademark gusto and grin. The novel was Charles Bukowski's Post Office.

Now here was something unlike anything I had read up to that point. It revealed a whole new approach to the art form I was so in love with. And like all great Art it was of its time. It took the best of what had come before it and forged something new. This guy took us to places none of the others dared to go or even could go. He was one of us. Blighted but gifted with a corruscating craft. There was a raw beauty within its brutality. It spoke the truth and pulled no punches. No sugar coated sentences.

Chav Punk Hobbit reads with the familiarity of some of the 20th Century's most irreverent and anarchic writers. They have a ghostly presence within the pages but no more than that. The story is strongly fixed with humour and the indulgent joy of surreal detail and through the authors unique vision the ordinary encounter is polarised into an extraordinary and compelling vignette. The prose is swift and spontaneous and at times starkly beautiful.

Of course this book is about a pilgrimage. It is an odyssey of spiritual enlightenment during a period of personal turmoil. In that sense it is vintage Jason. Dry aged oak barrelled Jason. Absurd and poignant in equal measure. Pirate thirsty for new experience and a deeper understanding.

This is a truthful travelogue from the Bukowski of Brynmawr. It is a simple tale. It is courageous and it is of our time.

Cai Hughes

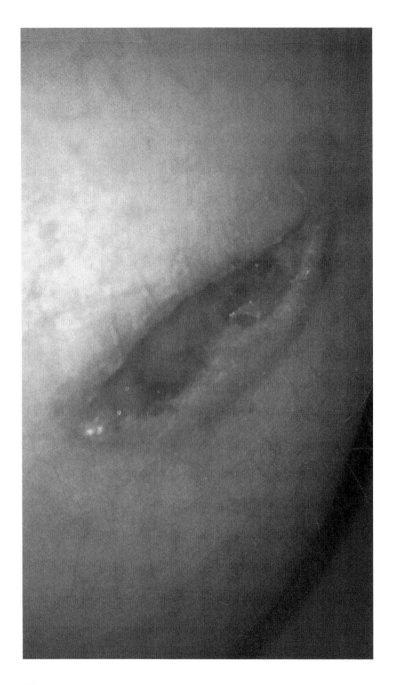

INTRODUCTION

SICKNOTE @ Freekuency April 2012

Baggage: all to fuck.

Plane lands at Porto. Five hours looking for an apartment.

Johnny No-Cash, drunk, attacks Lionel. Filth attacks Johnny. Bleeding Scalp. Everyone turns on him.

Smashed. Walk round Porto. Beautiful.

Meeting with Chloe, the new manager. Results as follow: website's shit, gigs are shit, fees are shit, merchandise is shit, everything's shit. Time to change? All agreed.

Off to the festy!

Mental ... Magic ... Munted ... Blur ... Abuse ... Memory loss.

Scrumpy. Powder. Pills. The Caravan. Chugging on a dildo with a moustache. Stabbing Johnny in the face. Filth's leg eaten by a rabid dog. Chloe tells everyone to fuck off. Doghouse loses voice and sprouts five cold sores. Dr Conker in bed with an alsatian. Spartacus on a leash after lamping people.

Crates of lager. Nostril fluff. Then on stage ... Three hour set. Were we possessed? Or just completely off it? Back to the caravan. More muntedness ...

Back to Porto. Sober Up. Wash. Huge meal. Looked up the info on the Camino Portugues.

Goodbye guys ...

DAY 1 : Goodbye

Porto - Vilarinho: 26km

The boys fumbled round packing their bags and twenty minutes later the front door clicked shut and a massive silence swallowed me whole. Was I scared? For a moment, YES. Then I walked round the flat naked and sat in front of the window. 4:00am. Emerging from the blackness, a huge lit up bridge and sprawling ancient city with a winding black silk river and bobbing boats stocked with barrels of port. I was on the side of a mountain, in a throne with my feet hanging out of the window.

I felt amazing. I wanted to stay. Right here. To write an album and suck up this amazing city. I could live here, I thought. I went back to bed as I'd only slept for about two hours. I couldn't sleep. My mind was racing about what the fuck I was going to do now I had been left in Portugal with very little cash and no plan.

I jangled the key towards the shopkeeper. That was it: I was gone. The flat was no longer mine. I was out in the open with nowhere to sleep tonight..

I got to the internet café, dosed up on some caffeine and sent a load of emails to delegate all of my Sicknote duties, for good. Time to let go. I emailed the Missus saying how much I missed her and downloaded the latest episode of Kenny fucking Powers.

The clock struck midday. I found the beginning of Camino Portugues and took my first step along the Way to Santiago ...

I was warned not to walk the first part of the Way and to get a Metro out of the city as the walk was dangerous and not very scenic. Still, I winded my way up the steep streets and loved it all: the cathedrals; the tiny streets with towering, almost derelict apartments stacked up on each other, with the occasional old round wrinkly spud-like man smoking out of his window or a similar looking woman flapping a blanket out of hers; techno with accordion and trumpets pumped out of some windows. These buildings were stacked up miles around and looked like they were ready to fall. Tiny scruffy kids kicked footballs around me and mopeds sped up and down the tiny streets. The way took me up out of the city and out onto some long, boring, busy roads that stretched for miles. I walked on as the sun beat down on my head.

Finally I was out of the city and surrounded by new scenery: a huge old house made of mud with tiny windows, within a lush, green, bumpy field with chickens, geese and goats. A stunning river glistening at me and pouring into a waterfall just beside me, which bumbled under the old wooden bridge I stood on.

I passed a man who was smoking and scratching his balls. His mouth was upside down, his nose like a deflated balloon. Four drooping eyelids sank below his chin, all hanging from his yellow, malnourished head. His trousers were up round his tits, which hung over his waist apologetically, supported by a woolly blue tucked-in jumper, just like Dr. Conker's.

"BOOTAR!"

He grunted back and nodded. I walked on and approached another busy road. I waited for a gap and launched myself across the road. A huge truck swerved as I straddled the central reservation, then I darted across.

I looked back, the man appeared to be playing with his todger. More and more furiously. He waved. I looked at him and he looked at me and just fiddled with himself. I shouted "What the FUCK are you doing?!" The traffic was darting between us.

He now appeared to be wanking in his scabby brown trousers and beckoned me. I escaped up a lane, laughing to myself.

Hours and hours passed with the sun beating on me as I followed the way of the Pilgrim. I passed one refuge but decided to keep walking as the way was so nice and sunset seemed a long way off.

16

After five hours of walking I met two German pilgrims and had a chat with them. They seemed tired and grumpy. I could see why as this was a long walk, with not much happening for miles.

I hit a horrible country road where maniacs in rusty, battered motors sped both ways; almost killing me on every bend. After another two hours of this nightmare I found a home with a sign swinging outside: "PILGRIMS WELCOME".

LUXURY! Power shower, internet, kitchen, double bed, en suite, garden.

I showered my aching, weary, sweaty body. Then I collapsed on the bed and Skyped my lady.

Was 236km, now:

210km to Santiago!

DAY 2 : Burning Soul

Vilarinho - Rates: 11km

"Bon Camino!" said Amidou as he shook my hand firmly, grinning.

"Ciao Ciao! Danke!" I replied.

I strolled through and out of Vilarinho up some lanes, sun warming me through, with a smile on my face. The Way took me through miles of silent farmland, with dogs barking in the distance and the occasional tractor or old, spudlike farmer looking at me as I passed. "Bootar", some would say ...

After a couple of hours I hit a eucalyptus forest and was taken through it on dry paths and roads. The wind began to pick up. The huge trees, all silver and skinny, creaked over my head and leaves rustled violently. Dust blew in my face and the sun kept warming the back of my neck.

After a good while I hit the town of Rates and got a bed at the Albergue. No costs: just donation.

9:00pm. A bell tolled. I was called outside with all of the other pilgrims. There were six older Germans and a Portuguese couple and the guys who ran the Albergue with their baby. The husband, who smiled all the time, poured various things into a large ceramic bowl which included alcohol, coffee beans ("boons", as the Germans called them) and several other ingredients. In the still, dark silence of the night, he set the potion alight.

He stirred it with a large ladle and lifted the blue, flaming liquid out like a fireball with the spoon. He then dropped it back, trailing streaks of blue into the burning bowl. He spoke softly and explained that this was an ancient Ritual named "Queimada". He said it was for burning away our sins. We sat there in the cold as it burned and he stirred and stirred. He asked us each to take a turn to stir and say a few words in our native language.

They all spoke. I poured the burning liquid back in and out

of the bowl. Why was I so scared of talking in front of people? My body shook. I told them I didn't understand a word anyone had said, told them of my band going home and me beginning my journey in Porto and thanked the hosts for their hospitality. We sat in the cold for an hour and I got talking to a lovely older German lady called Geezer (or possibly Gisa), whose English was better than mine! She wore her sleeping bag on her head and talked of her adventures. I was interested but in the end far too cold to be sociable.

199km to Santiago!

DAY 3 : The Ceremony

Rates - Barcelos: 16km

Carrier bags rustling. Too early. Need sleep. Please pack your bag elsewhere! Rustle. Rustle. Zzzzzzzip. Rustle. Zzzzzzzzzzip. Almost an hour or more; rustle, rustle, parp, rustle, zzzzzzzzzip, cough, whisper, zzzzzip, right next to me. Shhhhhhhhh.

I woke up and everybody was gone. I walk to the bathroom and smile at the cleaning lady.

"Rabalabalabalabalaaa! Noooo!" She said, throwing her arms around.

"Um, no idea, morning!" I replied.

In the mirror I look tired, hair stuck straight up like a shrub, eyes sagging and pained. I need more rest. I'm in bad shape. I must keep in mind I am still on a comedown from Freekuency Festival last weekend, so should go gentle on myself.

The sun didn't come out and the cloudy day just lingered on and on. My feet were in agony. I realised that these trainers I had blagged off Stevie G were totally unsuitable for walking over 200km and was in desperate need of my boots, which sat in my bedroom back home. It got worse and worse, each step sending pain shrieking right up into my brain.

After many hours of painful steps I arrived in the stunning town of Barcelos and all I needed was rest. I could walk no more. I sat in a large empty church for a while. When I gathered some energy I tried the Albergue, it was closed. No life. Nothing. I just needed a bed. Six hours of walking in the cold had got me. My feet were hurting bad. I was ready to lie down and sleep.

"OheeoOeOOeOOeeeeOoo" bellowed a large man at the black gates of the albergue. I could work out he was trying to tell me the people weren't there today, purely by the way he moved his body and face.

"Merci! Merci!" I replied

"Pas Normal! Pas Normal! Pas Normal!" he said, then hopped in his car and sped off.

I walk to the outskirts of town.

"Albergue?" I ask a passing lady.

She looks at me, baffled for a few moments.

"Ah!" she exclaims and points at a McDonalds. Jesus.

At this point I remembered having left a bag of food in the church, so I go back to get it. The place is in mid-service, all the seats full and rammed with people standing. I locate my carrier bag under the seat I sat in earlier, near the front. I go to grab it and a woman starts screaming at me and tapping the guy who is sat in my seat, thinking I'm stealing his bag. Half the congregation look round as she squawks, shaking the confused man in front. I stroll down the side aisle with about 150 people staring at me, half expecting a priest to rugby tackle me as I head down to the river to scoff my sardines and cheese.

It was getting late and cold, and I was fucked. After bartering with the lady in a hotel and getting her down from twenty-five Euros to twelve, I collapsed in a heap on the bed.

I woke up at 10:00pm in the tiniest room, but it was warm, cosy and no one farting next to me.

A huge, fuzzy full moon stared at me as I walked out of the hotel. It was set low in the sky next to a large, ancient fountain and to my left stood a huge old square church with bulbous spires.

The town was very busy for so late in the evening. One thing I noticed about Portuguese people is that they all have either completely black hair, or completely white hair. I got some strange looks probably because, for some reason, I seemed to be one of the only people in Portugal in their twenties or thirties. My hair was a golden mess of matted curls that sat on top of my head like a battered birds nest. I wore a cheap rain mac with baggy combats.

I couldn't work out why there were so many people around. In the distance I heard a faint drum beat.

Dum, dum, dum te DOM!

Following the army of drummers was a march through the old town; some kind of religious thing. Girls all in black with rattles, faces covered, with rope around their foreheads. Figures in black Ku Klux Klan style costumes, monk-looking types, priests, popes, kings, warriors, holy men, soldiers, then more women in black hoods, hundreds of them with candles in glass boxes on sticks. Then came groups carrying what appeared to be coffins. Young men dragging crucifixes. Other soldier-type groups carrying huge upright crucifixes on beds of flowers. Other groups of men carrying tall effigies of the Virgin Mary. No-one smiled. Maybe a thousand people marched in these dark, twisted, fucked-up costumes throughout the streets of Barcelos, following the slow beat of the death march: Dum, dum, dum te DOM.

It felt like the end of the world. They marched on, real slow, pausing on every left step. The rain began to fall. The beat echoed around the cobbled streets of the town and was all that could be heard. I followed them back up to my hotel.

Good Friday innit? That's it. A totally unplanned Easter Pilgrimage to Santiago!

185km to Santiago!

DAY 4 : Burning Sole

Barcelo - Tamel: 9km

Outside it was grey and miserable like a typical day back in Wales. The rain held off though, so it was dry, but I could feel the cold biting at me under the duvet. My feet squealed in pain as I took the three steps to the toilet. I checked out at midday.

Each and every step I took felt like an electric shock.

"No!" said the miserable skinny man.

"Menu?" I asked. "Mange? Food?"

His head was like an ice cream cone with tiny features placed on it. Just a tiny frown; a parsnip nose; a small, sad, pointless mouth; and then a slick, shiny Hitler hairdo swished over the top of it all. The ice cream cone was placed within a perfectly ironed shirt collar, over which he wore a perfectly ironed jumper tucked into perfectly ironed chinos with black slip-ons. This guy looked seriously unhappy and slid about behind the counter, drying glasses and trying to ignore me.

A microwaved pizza and beer, the clouds stirring overhead and the unfriendly people looking over at me as I was writing out my postcards made me wish I never fucking stopped here. Pricks.

"CIAO!" I belted out as I left, still chewing the shit cold food.

Up, through and out of Barcelos. Only a short day today, I keep thinking to myself, each step fucking ripping my soul and my soles to shreds. Then I begin to climb a mountain.

Portuguese chav kids look at me oddly, like they wanna mug me. What have I got? A sleeping bag? They probably think so. Little do they know I've got my Apple Mac in me sack! More of them in their little cars, wheelspinning. Then dogs flying at me, barking like they wanna tear me up with their rabid jaws, stopping a millimetre from my nose with a CLINK! and a YELP! as their chain tightens and they are sent flying back to their home. Loads of the fuckers. They all hate me! Thank the lord they're chained up. The sky darkens more and more and

the SHORT walk seemed to be taking forever …

"ALBERGUE?" I ask an old, tiny woman.

She holds up four short, brown, peeling fingers with no nails on them.

"KILOMETER??????" I ask.

"No, no. Minutos!" she croaked through her last black tooth. She pointed vertically up the hill and cracked a smile that would scare the shit out of Beelzebub.

"AHHH. BELLISSIMO!" I shouted nervously and ploughed on. Bellissimo? That's fuckin' Italian innit?

After another hour of hill climbing, I fall into the Albergue like the Hunchback of Notre Dame. On smack. After hiking Everest. In ballet shoes.

Can I go on? Fucknose …

176km to Santiago!

DAY 5 : The Resurrection

Tamel - Pont de Lima: 25km

I lobbed half my shit in the bin and headed out into the blistering sun at 9:30am.

Strolling down the other side of the mountain I realised my feet were healed. No pain. How? I was beaming.

Through the trees I could hear a band playing in the distance, like happy Christian music. More pops in the distance, too. Gunfire? No idea. It had woken me this morning, along with the blaring church bells and cockadoodledooooo!

POP again. POMPF! Pumpf! Pop. Over a large stone hump bridge with no sides and onto a vast, dry, empty landscape I strolled, mountains surrounding me at a distance and no clouds. Then more POP! Pompf! Popopop! Fireworks! Innit? Easter Sunday! That's it! They're celebrating the Resurrection!

Suddenly I felt amazing. Everything seemed perfect. It was like the first day of creation. Like everything had just been born and were all celebrating. I stretched out my arms wide in the perfect sun and screamed "FUUUUUUUUUUUUUCCKK YEEEEEEEAAAHHHHH!" It echoed for miles off the mountains, but there were no people in this empty new world to hear me.

I imagined a God on a huge analogue mixer in the sky. He created the perfect mix. The sound of nature. A blend of over-excited twittering birds, distant band coming over the land to me, fireworks popping off each of the surrounding mountains, the vibrating sun beating down on me and just my steps gently crunching into the ground. With feet that felt good. It was all there. Perfect. The Resurrection. I was back. Life is fucking great.

The Way took me up north towards Spain and managed to wind between all of the various mountain ranges so I never actually climbed, but followed a level route in between the valleys. The fireworks continued. My mouth began drying up

in the heat.

Time was passing. Hours and hours. I was still going. No shops. No cafes. Blistering sun … I needed to drink water. This was dangerous. There'll be one soon, I thought. There is every day. Cafes everywhere. But Easter Sunday? Hmmm …

I was heating up and turning red. Gasping for liquid to be poured down my neck!

I started to think of why I was doing this Camino. People have said you clear all your sins and are granted one wish on your walk. The last Camino I had dedicated to the health and well-being of my parents. But why the fuck was I walking to Santiago again?

I began to think about what I wanted. Money? A car? Shoes! Um, fucknose. What do I want? Dosh. Yeah and other shit. All these things. Lots of stuff. Um, A huge list! My thoughts wandered and I tripped out for hours. I concluded that the Universe will not supply money as it an unclear desire: what is the money for? Nor will it provide material things. It is not the language of the Universe. It will, however, respond to desired experiences. This is the language it understands. Our purpose is to EXPERIENCE and feed back to the Master Brain - the Universe - who is also the Creator. So, it might provide money or things to fulfil a desired EXPERIENCE! Aha!

'Am I losing my mind?', I thought, trapped in this huge odd bubble of solitude. At this precise moment, through the mad silence, a cuckoo cuckooed in a nearby tree.

I entered a wood and was strolling down a dusty path when the greenest lime coloured moth fluttered up to me and behind my head. Pure lime green. Moth? No, they come at night. Butterfly? But it looked like a moth. The lime was the limest lime ever. It reminded me of lime flavoured Calippos: those ice lollies. I so wanted a lime Calippo right now. Fuck YES! The ultimate quench! I used to love those things in the summer. Fuck, I could taste the butterfly. I was hallucinating with my taste buds! The lime-flavoured buttermoth then came flying back down in front me, now joined with a perfect, brilliant white friend: vanilla flavoured buttermoth! I was imagining the taste of them. Too much time alone and dying of thirst can really fuck with your brain. I put my theories to test and asked the Universe in that moment for an experience: "The best quenching of my mouth I could possibly get NOW! NOW!"

BANG!

Instantly I realised the carrier bag I had been carrying in my right hand – all day – contained a pear! I ripped it out and ate the shit out of it. I made love to the pear with my mouth and it was indeed the most amazing quench I have ever had. It dripped all over my face and I slurped it all up like a maniac and flicked the tiny stalk into the woods.

The fireworks kept on popping.

For lunch I sat on a slab of stone under a shady roof of purple flowers, next to a tiny babbling brook with geese looking down from a garden at me: the perfect pilgrim's rest. I ripped open the bread I had picked up earlier, that someone had left out for pilgrims. The lime green and vanilla buttermoths came back, right up to my glasses and fluttered over my face, gently fanning me, then flew up and beyond me. Purple blossom fell onto me and the tomato I was cutting with my bank card. I stuffed my face. Somehow the sardines from the tin seemed all wrong in this perfect scene.

I walked on for more several more hours.

"Agua! Eau! Water! Leeequiiiid!" I squealed over a gate at a lumpy woman sat on a step. She was surrounded by four crispy old women in wheel chairs. They all pointed down the street and started shouting some shit.

Around one more corner, was it a ... ? No. Hang on. YEEEAAA! I slapped my head straight into the drinking fountain, sucked the water right down to my deepest innards and panted as I tried to get more in quicker! At Last! GULP! Splash! PUFF! Pant! Suck! Gulp!

Lowering into a clearing, a wide river opened up beside me. A beautiful old bridge spanned across it in the distance.

Lots of cars and humans seemed to be gathered here. Barefoot by this point, hair everywhere, Poundland shades, chunky headphones and a tight white sweat-ridden T-shirt with "Benefit Cheat" logo on streeetched across my chunky torso. People everywhere. Everyone staring. All strolling about. Well dressed in shirts and shoes. Serious. Looking me up and down. This was Pont De Lima and was a quiet, beautiful town FULL of people! All looking at me. Everyone I passed.

Bow down, mother fuckers! The Chav Punk Hobbit has arrived!

Each old lamppost in the town and across the old arched bridge had been fitted with speakers that were playing Frank Sinatra. So, laid, back. If it was any more laid back it would BE the horizon. People looked like they couldn't be arsed. Nothing mattered to these people. Stress clearly did not exist here. They looked me up and down and carried on doing fuck all. And it slowly dawned on me. Yes …

I was the tallest person here!

I stand at 5' 5.5". I'm used to being amongst the shortest in any given situation and in a way I quite like it. But everybody here … was shorter than me! Yes, everyone I passed was shorter! And all overweight! Chubby. And the place was rammed: all across the bridge, everywhere. All celebrating the Resurrection and strolling around in their Sunday best. Even the tall ones were short and even the skinny ones had three bellies. Usually things grow towards the sun, but it seemed as if this lot had cowered away from it, hid in the mud like potatoes and just plumped up underground. And Easter Sunday was their annual day out. Everyone strolled about under the quiet popping of the fireworks and Sinatra. I looked like a strange white Shrek crossing the bridge between them all.

Then I spotted it. Someone eating a lime Calippo!

I sat on a small island with my fat feet in the river, sucking on my lime Calippo. The sun began melting down over the bridge as the little people strolled above me and "I Did It My

Way" come quietly seeping over the bridge to me.

Fireworks kept popping till sunset.

In ditching all my belongings this morning I was wrong: not all of the Albergues supply blankets. I put on every item of clothing I had and sank into a deep sleep.

149km to Santiago!

DAY 6 : The Astronomer

Pont de Lima - Tui: 42km

I thought Day 4 was a mountain. It was a mere speed bump in comparison to what I was now hanging off by my fingernails. I had to use all of my limbs to scale up the side of this beast. It went on and on; a big rocky gash up the side of a huge mountain. I guess it was inevitable at one stage I would have to cross one of these mountains. It just so happens it was the biggest fucker in Europe!

After three hours of dangling off this cliff, I finally scraped myself to the summit in a dusty pile of tears, sweat, blood and blisters. This was possibly the biggest climb I have ever done. Just before I began to scale the mountain I was talking to an elderly Canadian lady named Marie; a short lady with a saggy white neck and a tortoise head dangling under a floppy hat.

She smiled and strutted along all hunched over, as we walked together for half an hour.

"If I have one pearl of wisdom for you," she said, "this would be it: money comes and goes in life. Don't preoccupy yourself with it too much. Get a little cushion so you are safe and forget about it. The only thing you need to make sure you do is always do what you love. If you don't love what you are doing, stop doing it NOW."

I slid down the back end of the fucking volcano and reached a stunning village in a beautiful valley with several Roman bridges all covered in a creamy silence. I stood in a field with my pants round my ankles, slappin' on some Savlon. A big, burly bull nodded and mooooed its approval.

I sat at the end of a little stone bridge to take a break. I opened my bag to discover the eggs I (par)boiled this morning had broken all over my stuff. Then I found a lone sausage at the bottom of my bag. Lunch! Yummm!!!

"Snoooooooooorrrrrrrrt!!!!!!!! Sccchnnnoooooooort!!"

I slowly looked up. A black pot-bellied pig stared right into my eyes. I jumped up to my feet in shock. Still chewing on his relative, I packed my gooey bag up and got moving. It was early. My pace was fast as my strength was building everyday.

I drank a coffee and ate locally made chocolate with Jonas: a super fit young German guy who I saw in the Albergue last night. He was a friendly kid, only twenty years old. We chatted in the shade for a while.

An old, fat man walked past, not bothering to acknowledge us. He wore a rucksack on his back; another on his belly; an umbrella; a compass; several other gadgets and things hanging off him, swinging everywhere; floppy hat; and specs. We laughed at the sheer amount of shit he was carrying and how slow he crawled in the baking sun. We chilled in the friendly cafe a bit longer.

"Wanna walk?" asked Jonas.

"Nah you go ahead. I'll relax more. I'll see you on the way." I like to walk alone.

"How far to the next Albergue?" I shouted across the road.

"INGLESE?" bellowed the fat man who was now sprawled across a step in front of a church. Bells rang around us and cars whizzed between us. He was very wary of me and scooped his belongings in close to him. He then loosened up and shared his map and info with me as I lay down across the steps next to him.

He looked just like Patrick Moore from The Sky At Night and he sat there surrounded by maps, water bottles, mountain charts, rucksack, day pack, compass, watch and all sorts of shit.

"Ze next Albergue is Balenka, approximately eighteen kilometers, but I weel walk to España today."

What an amazing accent. German? South African! I have fallen in love with this accent since discovering my fave band of late, Die Antwoord. I couldn't get enough. My fave word he would say was "Yes". If you have ever seen the Scottish hotel owner from Little Britain you know what I mean.

"You walk to Spain today?" I asked.

"MmmMMMMyyyEeeeeeeeeeeeeeaaaatttcscsssshhhh!"

Wow. I now tried to get him to say "yes" as much as possible. "Really?"

"Mmmyyyeeeeeeeeeeeeeaaassshhhh!"

He offered me to walk with him. We completely lost track of all the yellow Camino arrows and deviated from the Way for the first time since Porto. We strolled down a super busy road as he spoke stories and history, legend and spirituality at me. Lorries whizzed past his rotund collection of flab, skin, belongings and brains.

Thomaas. An astronomer. Sixty-six years old. Walked 12,000km. 12,000! Born in Germany. Grew up in South Africa. He left because of the violence in 2004. He had six university degrees. Lived alone in a small village in Spain. Didn't speak Spanish and appeared to hate the Spanish. In 2006 his last living relation, his brother, a university lecturer, was murdered in his own home in South Africa by a gang who had broken in using brute force, shot him in the head at close range and stole his … fuckin' laptop.

"What do you think of Santiago?" I asked.

"Mmmmyeaarsh. A pile of tourist fuckin' sheeeeeit. I only go there because it is zee End!"

"Oh?"

"But, you must go on to Finesterra. A three day walk to the west coast. Finez … Finish … Terra … Land! Zee End of Land. You must walk there and end your Camino there!"

He talked of the history of The Camino.

"Santiago. Saint James,", said Thomaas, "The first apostle of Jesus. Yeeeeeeeeeeaaaaarrssssh! He was murdered! In Palestine. His remains were brought back to Santiago by his apostles. Seven hundred years later a monk claimed to see James in a vision. From then many people began the Camino de Santiago de Compestella."

He tested my knowledge on a range of subjects as we walked together for hours in the Sun. He shook his head and held it in his hand in disappointment at my lack of knowledge, mainly on history but many other subjects.

"Zew must learn your history about where you from come! YARZZZ!"

He filled my head with stories. I loved every single minute of it. Especially the YYYYYYYYEEEEEEEEEASSSSHHH bits.

"Jason? Hmmm," he said, "Yeeeeeeaaaaasssshhhh. Ziss reminds me of St. Christopher. The Saint of Travelling. Yaarse. They have similar stories of helping people. With Jason it was un old ugly hag. She was at the river begging for him to carry her across. Jason did indeed carry the ugly hag across and safely to the other side. It turned out that the hag was Hera, The Queen of Gods in disguise! She was the Goddess of Women, Marriage and Birth. She rewarded him for his generosity. Jason in search of the Golden Fleece. Hmmyeaaashh. In his mission he did not judge people and gave everyone a chance."

"How did she reward him?" I asked.

"I don't zememba! Doez not matter!!!"

He bought me a coffee and said "Right Jason. What is

coffeeee?"

"A bean?"

"Continue!" he snapped and looked toward the floor, waiting for me.

"Um … caffeine?"

"Yeeeeeeeeeeeaaasssssshhh, what else?"

He filled me in on the details of coffee and how it helps prevent skin cancer. He made me throw my Poundland sunglasses in the bin: my eyes are very important and these cheap glasses tricked my eyes into thinking it wasn't bright, thus opening them up to let in very dangerous UV. He told me to visit an eye specialist when I got home and to up my sunscreen to factor 50 immediately.

"If you are to remember one thing from me," he declared, "let it be this: The Law of Unintended Consequences. You never know what will come of what you do. So, get actively interested -in something! Pursue it. See where it takes you!"

He advised me to go to university immediately to learn and said I would be surprised by what would come from the people I met. He also told of the way he accidentally made his fortunes and ended up as a lonely astronomer in Spain, in love with the Universe.

"MmmYeeeeeeeeeeeeeeeeeeeeeeeaaaarrrrsssssssssscch!!"

We walked across the Eiffel Bridge as the Sun set. Leaving Portugal behind we approached the ancient town of Tui (pronounced Too-ey) in Spain. My legs were very tired and my right calf had seized and tightened up. 42km must be the longest I had ever walked in a day. I wondered how he must feel at 66 with all that luggage and 12,000 Km on the clock.

Halfway across, my mind blurred with happiness and exhaustion. I climbed over the edge and slowly pushed myself off the chunky iron bridge with my big toe. I thrust myself backwards, screaming, with my cock out, limbs a-flailing, speeding backwards towards the huge gushing river.

I ripped my clothes and rucksack off in mid-air. Thomaas looked over in bemusement. I fell for several minutes looking up at the sky and Thomaas and the huge bridge. My back slapped the freezing cold water and I rejoiced, travelling miles down in the clear river. There were mermaids and hags. And St. James and St. Christopher! And Marie and Jonas. Mr Eiffel! Sicknote! Stevie G! My family! Phil n Jill! Norris! Hera, the Queen of Gods! Jesus! All my school friends! A big whale! All of us swimming and smiling! Then my beautiful girl was there, all naked and pale, smiling, huge brown eyes wide open in the clear water. Her pert perfect little tits, white skin, huge brown hair, lush little belly and long legs and arms flapping towards me excitedly. We kissed and fucked in the depths of the river surrounded by everyone I had thought about in the last week in my loneliness. This must be underwater love.

"A bit of pain makes you more spiritual!" snapped Thomaas at the other side of the bridge. We shook hands. He went to find a hotel while I climbed the ugly, cold, old town, surrounded by dodgy looking drunks and muggers. In the shittiest, ugliest and coldest Albergue I found an empty plastic piss-proof mattress and lay down without a blanket. I thought of something both Marie and Thomaas had said today: "If you are given a gift then it is your obligation, no your duty, to share it with the world." A symphony of smells, snores and squeaky polite farts filled the air. Darkness came over me and rain began to tickle the roof outside. Fuck.

107km to Santiago!

DAY 7 : Flat

Tui - Mos: 19km

I stood in a doorway as the rain pissed down. 8:00am and I had twenty-five cents in my pocket. My bank card had failed to work in every machine. Depressed. My TK Maxx jacket could wrap around my bag, protecting my laptop and I could just about squeeze my arms in, but the front was open so my belly got soaked. The rain kept pouring over the ghostly town.

The smell of warm coffee and bread wafted into my cold doorway. I just wanted to sit in the café, flip open the laptop and write. My new addiction. Wait for the storm to pass. But not even enough for a coffee. FFS. I looked down at my cold, white, wrinkled toe poking out of the hole in my soggy trainers. What the FUCK was I doing here? I dreamed of being entwined with my girl in bed in Wales, all warm.

FUCK THIS SHIT!

FUCK SPAIN, FUCK THE CAMINO and fuck this rain.

I trudged through muddy paths, squidging around the sides of puddles. My first day in Spain. Flattened dead frog. Flat rat. Flat snake! Why flat? Snails crossed my path. There was nothing enjoyable about this muddy trek, in monochrome silence.

"Ola!"

"Olaaa" replied the Spanish lady. I recognised her from Tamel a few days ago.

Her face burst into a friendly smile. Big eyes and a lovely Th thththth th Spanish accent.

Esther. Forty-one years old. Mum of three. Married to an older man. From Valencia. A lone pilgrim.

We kept on keeping on through the ugliest part of the Camino yet. We walked together through long stretches of industrial estates for ages. Lorries and puddles.

"Ah Jason!"

There, slumped on the side of the busy wet road in a heap …
Thomaas! I introduced Esther and he burst into a rant of how
much he detested the Spanish. Oh fuck … Off he went, from the
housing, the prices, the history, the people, the government, the
banks, the scandal, the Muslim roots, the fuckin' everything:
this guy hated Spain. Esther took it all in, a bit astonished, but
smiled and sat next to him and discussed his views. But WHY
DID HE LIVE HERE! He doesn't even speak Spanish!

I explained to Thomaas how I was lucky to get a place to
sleep last night as I only just scraped together the five euros for
the Albergue from the bottom of my bag and my bank card
would not work. He pulled out twenty euros and demanded I
take it. I tried to say no … I'm sure it will work in the next town
… but he made me take it.

"Just in case, you never know!" he said, "I don't want it back.
Pray for me. You young ones walk on now."

We scoffed our faces with tortilla and coffee.

"When my little boy wakes me up on a Sunday," said Esther,
"he tells my huthband he's not allowed to be married to me any
more and that it's now his turn!"

He would get into her bed and open her eye lids with his
fingers and tell her she was the most beautiful woman in the
world.

"Only when you have children are you grounded," she said,
"It feels complete when you have your children. It's the best
thing in the World. They complete you. No matter what else
happens."

We ordered a bocadillo to take in our rucksacks and Esther
demanded to pay and told me to keep Thomaas' money just in
case. The sheer generosity of these people blew me away.

I left Esther as I needed to rest, my calf muscle was playing
up and she was keen to make progress today. We hugged and
off she went. I rubbed cream into my leg and thought about
family and what it would be like to be a dad. The rain pissed all

over me. Then all of a sudden the sun burst out, like a massive orange Chewit in the sky: mental unpredictable weather. I hobbled on further with the warmth of the sun on my back. I sung and thought and hobbled more. Until I reached a lovely, tiny village called Mos.

The friendly bar lady couldn't fill my glass enough with the deep red wine. Kept on topping up as I wrote more and more on the laptop. It was worth carrying across countries, just because I could keep in touch with people who mattered to me … and I could WRITE! Here! This shit you're reading now! And I wrote and wrote. And wrote. Six hours. I wrote. Skyped my lady. Drunk. Feeling nice. Galicia reminded me of Wales. Chubby, friendly people who loved to drink and eat. Green land full of rain. It was like being in a weird alternative Wales where I could talk to my loved ones through a computer. The bar lady smiled, not a word of English. And she charged me next to nothing for the seven or eight glasses of wine I had devoured.

'Why are some people so generous?' I thought, as I slipped into bed at midnight, drunk and happy. 'It always seems to be people who radiate something special from within, with a certain carefree lightness about them. Like they are confident that there is plenty out there for them and everyone else. Generosity - such an amazing quality in a person,' I thought.

88km to Santiago!

DAY 8 : In The Moment

Mos - Pontevedra: 24km

The young Portuguese girl who snored like a wart hog all night had now stretched up onto her back legs and was blowing her trunk all over my sleep-deprived body. Then commenced the chorus of zzzipping and crunching fucking carrier bags for an hour: a ritual of the early morning in every Albergue.

I headed up a mountain with a new six euro, long brown umbrella arched over me as the rain just kept on pelting at me. Thomaas was right: the umbrella is essential kit. The rest of the suckers had huge plastic capes over them and their rucksacks, which stuck to them, making them cold and miserable. I popped on my headphones and dusted two hours of my French audio course, tricking myself into believing I could hold a conversation when I headed to France in a week or so.

I walked across the soft moist mountain, totally wrapped in a grey sprawling cloud that hugged me all day long. My feet were drenched, but the rest of me was indoors under my new brolly as I strolled through what was exactly like my home land of Wales. Hours passed. Wales, I thought. Pays de Galles in French. Gales in Spanish. Galicia is a Celtic country. Then you have Gallic language. Je suis Gallois. Galicia and Wales were so similar: so wet, so silly, so happy, so generous. In history we must be so closely related. A distant memory of Welsh meaning Foreigner? I promised to learn the history of the Celts and where I came from when I returned home.

Finally, after six hours, I found shelter. I cuddled up in a dry corner of a shed next to a big ol' horse turd and bit into my squashed bocadillo. The rain kept on pissing.

Next stop, a few hours later, a tiny church: a small dim refuge for soggy pilgrims. A group of candles flickered in the dark corner and above them on a spike was a wax sculpture of a head. It looked freaky. The flames licked at it below. I looked closer … Fuckin' 'ell, this was weird … This was a sculpture

of a head alright … only … hang on … it is! The head looked exactly like ME! I jumped back in fright at the discovery. HOLY FREAKING SHIT!

There is nothing freakier than encountering a small sculpture of your own head. I stood in silence in this tiny cold dark church on the side of the mountain in the pissing rain.

I thought through the rainy day about how walking in this terrible weather ripped me into the moment. I understood that I had to learn to appreciate what is. This was the point, I think. The whole point of my Camino: to learn to appreciate and stop wanting. Feeling thankful and being in the moment was the secret to really feeling alive and being happy, I thought. The Camino teaches you this. I had to experience shit times and really LIVE in them in order to appreciate the good times when they came. I tried hard to appreciate the cold and wet and I managed to smile through the monotonous day.

I hung out with a group of heavy metal Spanish pilgrims in the night and joined Jonas for some pasta with a can of tuna. 'Twas a tough, wet day and we were all glad of the heated flooring in the Albergue!

> "In our daily lives, we must see that it is not happiness that makes us grateful, but the gratefulness that makes us happy." – *Albert Clarke*

58km to Santiago!

DAY 9 : Not In the Moment

Pontevedra - Caldas de Reis: 22km

I woke up with the usual rustling 'n' zipping and instead of waiting for everyone to fuck off as I normally did to get some kip, I got up and headed out into the sun before the noisy bastards. I was so excited about writing that I flipped open Smaragda, my trusty laptop, in the first café I found and began to type furiously while scoffing cakes and cafe con leches.

After five hours I thought I'd better get a move on and headed out with my umbrella in hand, into the unknown again. I thought about what I had just wrote and wanted to change it immediately. I had more to say. And I wanted to change the way I had said certain things. It was live on the blog and people were reading it, but it was all wrong. Ah fuck ... I thought about it more and more and was obsessing with all I wanted to say.

I completely ignored my lessons that were rammed home during my seven-hour rainy onslaught yesterday: the lessons of appreciating the moment. The sun shined and I walked as quickly as I could. Kept on going. All I wanted was a Wi-Fi connection so I could edit my blog. Nothing for hours. More dogs on chains barked like rabid wolves at me through large gates. In my frustration I began to bark back at them. This only served to make them more and more angry and try harder to escape to eat me.

Three bars, two cafes, still no Wi-Fi. Today was getting on my tits. I just wanted to write. I ignored all the scenery and people and just kept trying to get there. Fuck the journey, get me to the WI-FI!

I started to drift off after a few boring hours and began to think of technical ability in creativity and how my writing and my music always seemed better when I just blurted it out with no respect for technique. It's far more important to capture the spirit of something, I thought, than to be technically brilliant at something. But, how do you summon this spirit? Spirituality.

It has to be the essence of something. I remembered Thomaas talking about how my hurting legs would make me more spiritual. So is Pain the creator of Spirit?

Then from around a corner came hurtling two dogs, on the loose. No chains. No gates. No protection for meee! FUCK! They came straight for me, going for one ankle each, their jaws salivating and barking like beasts from hell. I must admit, they weren't the biggest dogs I've ever seen. Ok, they were tiny. But that ain't the point! They were ANGRY and had something to prove! As if all the other dogs in the region had howled through the hills and communicated that I had been barking back at them all day. These little insane slippers-with-jaws were now ready to make me pay.

I flipped around my umbrella and swung it wide between them. They kept barking, it was becoming more of a roar, like an angry pair of bears or something. I starting shouting FUCK OFF YA CUNTS and other random abuse at them. Being Spanish dogs they probably had no idea what I was saying …

Another wide swing and as I brought the brolly up the fucker on the right darted for my ankle. I brought it down and clipped him on the end of his nose. He yelped a pussy squeak and darted off around the corner, his friend still roaring at me. I kept swinging the umbrella and screaming like a lady being attacked. He edged off backwards in the direction of his friend. My heart was pumping blood around my shaking body. I composed myself, muttering "Little fuckers" as I turned round to get out of there. I almost walked into a tiny Spanish granny who stood speechless, having witnessed me jumping round like a bellend with an umbrella, screaming at two chihuahuas.

"Olaaa!" I said.

"Ola" came the stiff, quiet response as I shuffled off.

CAFE! WITH WI-FI! Yay! Sat down. Served the biggest bocadillo known to mankind.

A bocadillo is basically a sandwich. A huge sandwich. Dry. No butter. No fillings except a thin piece of dried, dark red meat slapped in there. Like a rotten, minging tongue in the middle of a crusty old loaf. I gulped it down, trying to wet my pimply, dry, white mouth in-between bites with the miniscule cup of coffee.

I flipped open Smaragda the Laptop, ready to WRITE!

Two policemen walked in and my laptop started having a spack attack. Could it be their equipment, I thought? I waited 'til they went. The screen went nuts, like never before: letters and numbers all over the place, things going bananas. Then it just died.

OH. No.

Now, this is my instrument on stage with the band. It's made thousands of people dance and that's its main use. It's also my communication device for keeping in touch with people. My production tool. My accounts. My diary. My cinema. My bank. My porn beatermax. My typewriter. My Skype machine. My flyer maker. My video maker. My marketing machine. My library. My … my … my everything, basically. PLEASE DON'T FUCKING DIE!

I tried everything. I ended up with just a flashing question mark on the screen every time I tried to switch it on.

There was a big lesson for me to learn here. This happened for a reason and I knew it.

At the Albergue I drank lots of lager and was half asleep and half crying, draped over an arm chair as the familiar chorus of snores and guffs fluttered over me.

"Technique doesn't come into it. I deal in emotions."
– *Jimmy Page*

38km to Santiago!

DAY 10 : Nobody Gives A Shit

Caldas de Reis – Teo: 25km

Walking has a way of ripping you into the moment. Empty sparse landscapes, no people, nothing, alone. What you find, though, is that it's hard to think, as the simple repetitive act of putting one foot in front of the other and following yellow painted arrows across beautiful wet countries, forces you into the moment and empties your mind. Kind of in the way they talk about meditation, but this pulls you into the moment without any hippy non-thinking ability from you. It's a great place to be. All the important encounters of the day are filed away into separate drawers in your mind, at night just before you enter dream mode. This is the way it was supposed to be. Thinking can be bad for you!

And now the only thing that stopped me from being in the moment, my laptop … was dead.

This is it! The Universe was FORCING me into the moment. Really, the past and the future only exist in our mind. So by shushing your mind you are in the moment.

The Sun tried to peak out of the eerie Galician mist. Around a corner, a sunray beamed onto a rock next to a lovely, tiny waterfall where, munching through a slab of chocolate, sat Thomaas the astronomer!

I told him about my writing up of my Camino on my blog and how he featured in it.

"Eeeeers. Why bother?" he replied. "Nobody gives a shit! Your grandkids won't give a shit, your friends will be too busy to give a shit, I don't give a shit and in a coupla weeks you won't even give a shit! Eaars."

His excited Yes – "Yeeeeeeeeeeeeeeash!" – of the other day had calmed into "Ears". I told him of my laptop disaster and, thinking of his rant about how computers were fucking up the world the other day, thought he would respond with some negative quip. I was shocked to see genuine concern on his face as he tossed me a slab of chocolate.

"Is for you."

I scoffed the lot as I rubbed more cream into my bulbous, varicose-looking leg.

We tucked our brollies into the bucket by the door as a huge ball of a human rolled over to us and threw two bowls of piping hot soup onto our table. This perfectly round barman was hairy on his chins 'n' arms and slotted into oily dungarees that emitted a mouldy stench.

"Heil Hitler!" shouted Thomaas, throwing his arm in the air. The perfectly round barman and his three round friends stopped and looked over in shock, as Thomaas excitedly burst into an animated monologue about how the cabbage in our soup was popularised by Hitler and actually prevents cancer. "Yeeeeears. It's why we are called krauts!"

"I thought you were South African?"

"I am a citizen of Zee Universe! Ears."

Back into the relentless rain and for several more hours he spoke his special kind of fucked up wisdom at me.

How today was Friday the thirteenth and was one of the most common phobias, to the point where whole harbours of boats would not sail. It is known as Triskaidekaphobia.

Thomaas had been building up the importance of the Ulla River which we would pass today. This was the river that the angels and the apostles of Saint James pushed the stone tomb up to take his remains to Santiago. It was a biblical and ancient story and a sacred river. I looked forward to crossing it.

He spoke of Hannibal – the greatest military commander in history – and of how in about 200 BC he took thirty-seven elephants across Europe and over the Alps to shock attack Rome. Thomaas had retraced his steps on foot recently.

And about cutting the Gordian knot: a metaphor for solving tricky problems by cheating or thinking outside the box. How Aristotle's student Alexander had solved the knot problem. It was said whoever could untie the knot would rule all of Asia. Many tried and failed. Then Alexander the Great simply took his sword and cut straight through it.

He told me how history was written by the victors and therefore probably everything we knew was fiction, written to make the victors look good.

He also said how no real, great businessmen in history had ever made money a goal in their vision of changing the world.

I recalled a line from The Teachings of Don Juan: something about knowledge not being knowledge unless it has a use to you.

We stepped onto the bridge over the Ulla River and … well … um … The sacred river was … ugly. A big factory on the other side bellowed yellow smoke as the stinking river spewed its mess below us. It looked a bit like Newport where I grew up, but more desolate and desperate. Ugly. This was a shit hole.

"What makes you truly happy?" I asked Thomaas.

"Life is not about happiness   Jason. What is this preoccupation you have with Joy? Eeeeeears."

"Why are you walking the Camino?"

"I am a theologian."

I dared not tell him how, when he asked me to pray for him, I had asked the Universe to send him a lovely Spanish wife to show him happiness!

Through an empty, depressing fairground, then through rows of knobbly trees and then I sat on a wall in the dodgy town of Padron. My legs hurt and I was cold, shadows sloped behind corners eyeing me up. Thomaas told me he would leave me now and find a hotel and tomorrow we would arrive in Santiago, but statistically the chances are we would not see each other again. I rubbed my leg and moaned something about my laptop and he cracked a wicked smile and blurted out his favourite line – "It makes you more Spiritual!" – before he turned round and disappeared into the fog forever.

I decided to walk on out of Padron to the next town but it was getting late and just kept on raining. Finally, after another two and a half hours, I reached the tiny village of Teo.

I took a glass of the house red from a tiny woman in a tiny bar. The doors swung open like in cowboy films and in from the torrential black rain strutted a mysterious, dark, triangular-looking figure. Everything was pointy: his big white pointed quiff. His protruding pointy chin. His strong isosceles

nose. His goatee. His thin pointy moustache. His arms 'n' legs were tapered and even his torso was a equilateral triangle. His pointy boots finished off the pointy man.

He leaned on the bar, clicked his fingers and lit up a pointy cigarette. In a puff of smoke he threw back his triangular head, swigged down his wine and his pointed Adam's apple rose up to his chin and then dropped back down under his triangle collars with a gulp. Leo Vignola from Uruguay, now living in Galicia and playing the blues for a living. He demanded to buy me a drink and then took me to his house down the road: a crazy little place where a fire burner crackled in the gloomy, dusty den. He filled up a random bottle to the brim from a old, battered-looking barrel and whacked a cork in it with the palm of his hand.

"For your final day of the Camino!" he barked, with a wild, massive Dairylea grin … He looked like the singer from Gogol Bordello. He winked and shook my hand vigorously for about eight minutes, almost dislocating my shoulder, grinning and staring at me, winking occasionally.

At the Albergue I got drunk into the early hours with a German guy who looked like the Plasticine man Morph. He couldn't speak a word of English, but could sing "Jingle Bells" perfectly and jump round the room. This guy was happy and completely nuts.

13km to Santiago!

DAY 11 : Santiago

Teo - Santiago: 13km

Hungover. Everyone gone. I raided the fridge and headed out into the pouring rain.

Just thirteen kilometres today. Maybe I'll make the Mass at Santiago Cathedral.

I walked and walked and walked. Thirteen kilometres my arse. I hit the outskirts of Santiago and it kept on going. Where did these arrows finish? My feet were soggy and I was tired.

Crows circled the grey skies around the Gothic spirals of the cathedral. A nun sung spookily to a packed-out service. I shuffled through the people and slumped onto the floor with my smelly bag and dead laptop. I closed my eyes.

Was I supposed to feel emotional? I know when I arrived here in 2004 after walking the 800km Camino Frances, a tear rolled down my reddened cheek as the organ hit its first bassy chord. But today, after just eleven days of walking, I was feeling, I dunno … I guess the hangover didn't help. I was tired. Soggy. Pissed off. The huge, cold cathedral offered no warmth to my heart or soul.

"Jathon," whispered a voice, as a tiny hand touched my shoulder.

"Heeey," I inaudibly hummed as I just about turned round…

It was Esther, smiling her big Spanish smile. She looked refreshed and bent down to join the pathetic soggy lump that was me.

I couldn't be bothered to speak. All I wanted was a bed. A priest started chanting some weird, monk type stuff real quiet and a baby cried behind me.

"I'll meet you at 5:00pm by the cathedral entrance," was about all I could muster up.

Got a bed. TRIED to sleep. Some Italian guy had a one hour animated conversation with his mum on his iPhone, so happy he finished the Camino, crying … GRRR. So much for that …

The old town was nice but, yeah, I was stuck in a tourist trap. Everything was expensive. We talked lots of how Esther was lost and needed headspace to think things through. She had the perfect life back home, but for some reason was unhappy. She didn't know why. I was surprised as to how open she was. I wondered if all lone pilgrims were lost.

She invited me to dine with her at her hotel. It was the one next to the cathedral, five star. There were stretch limos out front and horses and carriages. Several wrinkly men in white robes were being escorted in. Women in gowns and diamonds. Men in suits. More religious-looking people in robes. And then an old dude draped in a purple curtain.

I weaved between the gaggle of rich weirdos with my toe poking through the hole in my trainer and my muddy combats tucked into my socks.

We ordered the finest food you can eat in Galicia, while a guitarist weebled sweet harmonics into the atmosphere between us. We gulped wine and talked and laughed. I ordered another vino as her husband paid for the lot on his credit card over the phone.

I spent the night listening to a guy sleeping on the bed above me snoring like a diplodocus with the flu.

I had made it. Santiago. This was it. I had arrived.

The destination didn't move me a great deal. Crazy walkers walked for miles to reach this place for centuries. But it's not the destination that matters, I thought. I had heard people along the Way say that the Camino could be a metaphor for life. Your life. And everyone must walk their own Camino. No two Caminos are the same. One thing ringed in my mind while lying here:

Make the most of Your Journey.

DAY 12 : Rest

I drank excellent coffee in a local cafe and sat there feeling lonely and empty.

The sun was trying to come out but the rain prevailed. From a small, beaten-up TV in the corner came a song by The Black Keys. The opening riff grabbed me. The song: "Lonely Boy". Epic chorus … It chimed through my being. It lifted me up out of my seat and I floated towards the TV, hairs pricked up. The box announced that the album it was from was 'El Camino'.

I strutted around the town and took it all in, "Lonely Boy" echoing in my mind. I located the Apple Store, where I was to take my dead laptop tomorrow. I bought a notepad and I planned my route out of Santiago.

I sat in the cathedral and took out the pad to see if I could write. I struggled to put words into order without a computer … This was not good. Candles flickered around the cold, orange room and quiet, echoey coughs barely reached me. I sketched and doodled for a while.

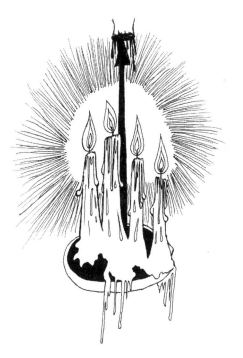

"Hallo?"

Jonas! We went for a few beers and then he had to go to take his flight back to Germany.

I headed for the Internet Cafe, did some more writing and talked to my girl. I left at midnight and headed back to the Albergue, looking forward to a good rest before the walk to The End of the World tomorrow.

I put my swipe card key in the door and a deep, ugly "bzzzzz" burped at me along with a RED LIGHT. I tried again … and again … and again. Again. Again.

The cold crept up and bit my love handle and a dog woofed in a nearby street. Shit. The lights in the bedroom upstairs were off. A lovely, warm, open fire sizzled just inside the front door.

Swipe. Bzzz. Swipe. Bzzzz. Swipe. BZZZ . Red fuckin' light. I knocked the door to see if anyone might hear it upstairs. I knocked harder and harder …

I got a number off the door and rang it in a phone box. Nothing. I knocked the hotel next door. A long guy with a candyfloss muff fringe dangling in his eyes came out and warbled at me.

"WHAT?"

I eyed up some bushes opposite, looking for somewhere to get my head down. I was freezing and it was getting late.

I was fuming. I kicked the fuck out of the door. No one could hear me. I walked up the street. A man with a Kinder Surprise head stood in the dim light, just outside his front door. He was in pyjamas and slippers, with specs and a pipe. He looked at me suspiciously.

"Albergue? Phone number?" I shouted at him across the street.

He looked at me blankly. I flashed my key at him. He shrugged, edged his way in and closed the door.

I edged my way up to the bush, eyed it up and wondered how the fuck I was going to get warm in it. And whether any rabid dogs might come and eat me. I was freezing. And angry.

Then, from across the street, a lady was heading for the

albergue door. She swiped her key.

"Beeeeep", GREEN!

"WAIIIIIIIIITTTTT!" I bellowed from the bush.

She looked petrified as I came hurtling across the road like a two legged bull. She stood frozen as I whacked my soggy, freezing foot in the door just as it was about to close.

"Hi," she said.

She recognised me from earlier.

"Hiya," I said, as I slipped passed her into the warm room and sank into a huge chair next to the open fire.

"Beer?" she asked.

DAY 13 : To The End of the World!

Santiago - Villaserio: 28km

I got up after everyone had gone and complained about the broken key. The hippy laughed, took me up to the café, offering me anything I wanted on the menu for free. So I ate everything I could possibly stomach.

"I am Apple expert. Please leave with me and I will email you in twenty-four hours."

His name was Angel. It was a sign! He spoke very little English but I left the laptop there and he gave me a receipt. I knew he would fix it. I would walk to Finesterra and be back to collect my machine in a few days.

I headed out into the baking heat, up through a university campus and up some woody hills. The sun pounded down on me. A fluffy ginger beard poking out of a flat cap strutted towards me. Its owner's limbs were alive with excitement and his extremely round eyes pierced me, as a cheesy white grin broke out of his beard.

"Excuse me. Where is the Camino to The End of The World?" I asked

"We are on it!" he sang, in a high pitched Irish lullaby. We shook hands and strolled on together.

Up over hills and out of Santiago, the Cathedral disappeared into the distance and the sun belted down upon us. We talked and talked. His name was Eoin (pronounced Owen). He had done the main Camino Frances, which I had walked before. We talked of our adventures and life and everything.

After a few hours we stopped at a bar and took a few beers in. This was a fucking great day. We smiled and walked. It was so easy: my bag was pretty much empty save for a few items of clothing and a pad. We walked through stunning old towns with a fat orange sun in the sky, rivers babbling below humped bridges. I told him of my disappointment in a situation back home where a "friend" had turned out to be a cunt and had not

only taken advantage of me but also left me in deep financial trouble. Eoin told me of a time when a "friend" had stolen his girlfriend and we talked of the repercussions of revenge and the lightness of forgiveness, letting go and looking forward.

We stopped at another café, took a beer and sat near a long, slinky Swedish lady who purred at us as we talked of our journey.

Eoin was keen to push on. I needed a bit of time. I swigged my beer as he slipped around a corner. After half an hour I plodded on, through the small town. There was an amazing statue of a man leaving his family, with the kid gripping hold of him, begging him not to go. I thought of my grandad leaving my eight year-old Mother in poverty and fucking off to Australia in the early 1960s. Forty years later he had come back to visit and keeled over and died in the very room where he had left his family.

I was determined to make some headway, but the sunlight was quickly disappearing. Cronky cars whizzed passed me. The sun paused for a minute and then suddenly flew below the horizon. Total darkness. Beady eyes flickered in the hedges next to me. I picked up the pace, launching myself towards the hedge when car lights were coming towards me. I could see nothing now and was sure I had missed the yellow arrows that showed me the way. I was cold, I was scared, I was unsure where I was or where I would sleep and almost certain I had lost the Camino.

As I walked on I realised I was walking towards a distant chorus of guttural dog barks. As they grew louder and louder, I grew more and more frightened. It was as if I was approaching the gates of Hell. And....... up ahead, I could make out the shape of a huge wolf. It was walking back and forth across the road ahead of me. HOLY SHIT … The freaky silhouette slinked around rolling its shoulders, looking cocky and its eyes lit up and flickered at me. FUUUUUUUUUUUUUUUUUCK!

I span around, immediately wheezing in fear and walked quickly back towards the last town. Two hours away, I think …

I walk for about five minutes, then stop and turn back towards the wolf at the gates of Hell, arse twitching like a burning moth. I cross to the opposite side of the spooky, silent road and walk as quickly and quietly as possible towards it. Only just holding in my wimpy cry as I approach the beast, he lays upon the floor, huge and white, barely visible in this dull dusk. I creep past, trying not to make eye contact, holding my breath. It rests its monstrous head on its paw and stares at me with his evil, luminous, orange eyes. He watches me all the way and does not move, while my heart goes BUMP BUMP BUMP BUMP BUMP BUMP. He must smell the fear emanating from me, but I pass and let out a huge sigh of relief. I slide down the steep, curvy bank of a road, heading towards the barking Hounds of Hell, fucking petrified of what lay ahead. Then a bar! Run for it!

"Hi, is there an Albergue nearby?" I ask.

"Here," said the bored, miserable bar-lady, barely bothering to open her mouth or look at me.

"THANK FUCK FOR THAT!" I squeal. I AM SAFE!

I pay for a wine and a room and the door swings open. Eoin! He perches on a stool next to me. We order a couple of omelette bocadillos.

"That's the best omelette sandwich I've ever had!" exclaimed Eoin, trying to force the dry shit down his neck with a gulp of wine. He holds his glass in the air with a smile, pauses and continues.

"That's the ONLY omelette sandwich I've ever had!"

The grumpy bar-lady taps her watch and ushers us out of the bar and we get into our beds. All the sleeping pilgrims moan about us arriving late and start shhhhhhing us.

74

DAY 14 : The Road Less Travelled

Villaserio - Olveiroa: 22km

I head into the morning rain with Eoin and a wrinkly American dude called Mike. They knew each other and were in deep conversation as I walked slightly behind them. Mike was arched over, equipped in military style regalia.

The three of us just walk and walk and walk. There are no shops. There are no villages. I let them go ahead for a few hours. The rain is relentless and there is nowhere to stop. We are gagging for some warmth and rest. Literally nothing but road. Hours and hours and hours. Just road and rain.

Eoin starts to lose it and runs down side streets looking for warmth or a shop and then catches us up again, shouting in anger. Mike must be in his seventies and is a total trooper: just keeps on keeping on with a wry smile and a knowing look. Inspiring! After maybe five hours of walking in the grey sheet rain, we spot a bar!!!

"Three beers and three steaks please!" I shout as we throw our wet shit on a hook. There were taxis pulling up outside and pilgrims getting in! Lazy cheating bastards! As tempting as it was to get in a cab and get to a warm bed, we knew this was not the way of the pilgrim.

We hit the wet road once again, got our heads down and went for it. In Olveiroa there were several small cottages with heating and a note saying to make ourselves at home. A lovely, homely Albergue in a tiny, lovely village. We hung our clothes about and the sun began to poke out. BIT LATE NOW!

It's still early and we all hang out, shower, lie around, read and get feeling good. Eoin got to work in the kitchen, showed off his culinary skills, cooked up a storm for us and I supplied some wine. We all headed down the local pub as the sun set. Feeling good!

We drank and sang and laughed into the wee hours and stumbled to our beds holding each other up and laughing more.

DAY 15 : The Darkest Hour

Olveiroa - Finesterre: 30km

Mike the wrinkly trooper was gone at the crack of dawn. Not before dropping all his money on the tiled floor and waking me up at stupid o'clock! I headed out shortly after. Shit … The rain was back. Twice as hard. I sat in the pub we were in last night and looked out of the window sipping a hot coffee. It was torrential and I did not want to go out there. A huge pink German girl came in and sprawled herself along the barstools. She had stayed in this pub last night and was just booking another night. Damn fine idea.

I walked to the end of the road and stood in a barn. Fuck this. No, I said. Come on. This is the End. The Beginning of the End. Come on!

I headed up the road as the rain pissed all over me, never letting up for one moment. I hobbled along thin paths, up and down the edge of mountains. Huge wind turbines swung majestically and silently in the distance, cutting through the heavy spooky mist. Water was everywhere. It was pissing down the path I walked on, pissing down the mountains I scaled and it pissed down the back of my neck, through my shoes and into my feet. There was no getting away from it.

As I tried to flap some shape back into my battered, soaking umbrella, a huge brown horse just over the fence next to me rose in the air like Pegasus! He screamed a painful yelp at me and started galloping and jumping around towards me. Was it was trying to escape? It seemed like he was trying to tell me something! Was he angry? Or just wanted to come with me? Or was he offering me a lift? Or warning me of something nasty that lay ahead? I began to quickly pace up the broken turquoise stone mountain path that swung from beneath me into the grey sky ahead. Sorry horse, I don't understand! What was wrong with him, I wondered? I panted up the hill, sure the horse was about to break loose and come and get me.

More hours of wet, windy, irritating walking. I have never experienced such bad weather. It just kept coming and the path kept extending over every brow I scaled. More grey. More stone. More steps. More solitude. More insanity. More wet. More pain. More spiritual. I couldn't stop as I feared I would slump to my death into a muddy puddle, only to be the plump dinner for a wild boar, or discovered in a few days by another lone pilgrim.

Suddenly, out of the grey horrid day an erect fat penis bounced in front of my face. A single bright pink, phallic flower swayed on top of a long green stalk in the wind, looking erect and a little threatening! The opposite of my shrivelled, beaten manhood … I felt intimidated by the flower cock. I rubbed my own freezing blue ruffle of skin in a pathetic attempt to try and make it 3D again. I knew I had to be a man now and this is what this cocky flower was trying to tell me …

More hours slipped by as I grinned and bore the wind slapping my face and the pain of this never-ending day. I was begging for a glimpse of the ocean to signal to me the end was nigh. When I finally started to descend, I could make out a coastal town with a huge factory bellowing more grey into the grey landscape.

"Would you like a lift?" asked a well dressed skinny man under a umbrella in the quiet town.

"Um, to where?"

"Up the hill there is a beautiful Albergue with hot food and lovely hosts," he smiled, pointing. It sounded like heaven. I had never been so cold or wet.

"Thanks very much, sir, but I'm a fucking pilgrim! I must walk to the end of the world," I said, through chattering teeth. He jumped in the air with excitement, laughed out a ladylike giggle and slapped my bingo wing.

"Owwww!"

"A true pilgrim!" he laughed. "The right answer! I was once

a pilgrim and when I noticed you there, looking as beaten as I once was, I thought I would test you!"

"Um, thanks … I think?" I replied.

"At the top of the next hill, stay in the Albergue! It is the finest on the whole Camino! With free hot food! You will love it! Good luck." He skipped off into the town.

It's so tempting, when things get tough, to just give up when we are so close, I thought. The hardest part is always just before the end.

I sat my grumpy arse in a coffee shop and arched my wrinkly hands over the coffee to try and defrost them.

"Jheeson!"

I spun around, a drenched and red faced Eoin stood there dripping, arms open wide. Puddles formed under our seats and smiles broke out on our cracked, soggy faces as brandy warmed our souls.

I realised now that if I had brought my laptop on this part of the journey it would have been completely ruined in this rain, so if there is a chance of it being fixed at least it's safe.

We head out and decide we are going to finish the Camino today, despite us being drenched, hung-over and completely beaten.

We walk and talk and battle through the relentless sheet rain and finally reach the Cape of Finesterra! We roll up our jeans, take our shoes off and enter the shallows of the massive arc of beach that leads to a distant lighthouse.

The scene is insane. It seems like we are in a picture. Even the sound seems surreal. The sea and the sky blend into one with an arc of dark grey sand extending out of the white waves. I cannot express our feelings as we walk the final steps to the End of the World. We are silent and this is right. A Welshman and an Irishman. Not one other human being. Walking through the Galician sea in the heavy mist. It just felt right: a deafeningly beautiful moment I will always remember.

The lighthouse seemed miles away, but we silently, slowly got there with the bite of the Atlantic Ocean on our battered

feet, making us realise it was not a dream.

As we walked up through the town, my head began to spin. I'd never felt this way before. I held onto a wall and dropped my trainers. The floor was reaching for my head. I was about to drop. Was the cold killing me? Was the beauty of the moment killing me? Was it exhaustion? I was going to faint. Eoin grabbed my arm and helped me take my final steps of the Camino barefooted, in pain, head spinning, but overcome with a delirious joy.

We were greeted by an animated woman with a bandana and red cheeks and several pilgrims, all shouting and screaming in a cold hall. I slumped my soggy soul into a plastic chair and buried my spinning cold head into my hands. She kept shouting and screaming about certificates.

"Name?" she asked

"Jason Phillips"

"Age?"

"35"

"Nationality?"

"Welsh"

"Starting point?"

"Porto"

"Occupation?"

"Retired," I replied.

This sent her into a frenzy of laughter, as she grabbed my cheeks and pulled them off my head. She bounced up, tried high-fiving me and everyone else in the room and kept repeating "RETIRED!" and laughing her arse off.

Finally I got in the shower. Eoin gave me a towel, a jumper and a cup of tea. I just could not warm up … I got into bed and thought I was going to die.

A few hours later I had stopped shivering. A nice London geezer lent me his size twelve dry shoes and I waddled to the pub looking like Pingu. We ate octopus and drank 'til the early hours in the corridors of the Albergue, singing and laughing with people from all over the world.

DAY 16 : The Beginning

I woke up before anyone else at the Albergue. I scribbled out a note in the cold quiet morning and slotted it under the pillow of the snoring Irishman.

I was being thrown around the back seat of a bus as I dreamed of France, my lovely lady, Wales, my band and what life had in store for me next. I felt as if I was travelling down the fallopian tube of Mother Nature, winding my way back through the most beautiful scenes I had passed on foot, ready to be spat out in Santiago to begin my new life. A strange excitement of the unknown smothered me.

I had struggled through a stunning quest to reach the End of the World. Although this Camino had ended, this was just the beginning of my new life. Bring it the fuck on.

Printed in Great Britain
by Amazon

32975868R00052